BIBLE BRIEFS

God's Will:

UNRAVELING THE MYSTERY

Endorsements

Finally! A bold and new level of Bible study for those with full schedules but yearning to better understand the heart of God. The rich and deep spiritual nuggets found in these Bible Briefs will provide a new perspective on your purpose, God's will, and how to live in it during this last season of our earthly journey. Let's be intentional about building God's kingdom and glorifying Him in all we do. Thank you, L.G., for being obedient in sharing these treasures that God has placed deep in your heart.
—Susan Olguin, vice president for an international ministry and fellow warrior for Christ.

If you're interested in a study that's perfect for ordinary people, you have just stumbled across a Bible study rich with mature, spiritually responsible wisdom. L.G. Westlake has written a casual, engaging study that is filled with vulnerability and honesty. You will discover how the familiar is often what we most often overlook, and how this study is deceptively simple. We often make things too hard! *Bible Briefs: God's Will—Unraveling the Mystery*, is a crucial study for those who are interested in fulfilling the Great Commission, and should be a staple for anyone who is called to the mission field.
—Travis W. Inman, author of the Earth Fire Series and the Glenfield Series

Uncovering the elusive will of God has been the subject of which many philosophers and theologians have written. But we've missed the beauty of the forest while examining the trunks of the trees. This study guides the reader back to the bigger picture of God's will and to the often-overlooked straightforwardness of His Word.
—Anne Gressett, Bible study leader

BIBLE BRIEFS

God's Will:

UNRAVELING THE MYSTERY

L. G. WESTLAKE

PUBLISHING THE POSITIVE
Plymouth, Massachusetts

Copyright Notice

Cover and Interior Design:

Editor(s): Mary W. Johnson, Judy Hagey, Deb Haggerty

PUBLISHED BY: Elk Lake Publishing, Inc., 35 Dogwood Drive, Plymouth, MA 02360, 2022

Library Cataloging Data

Names: Westlake, Laurie (Laurie Westlake)

Bible Briefs—God's Will: Unraveling the Mystery / Laurie Westlake

140 p. 23cm × 15cm (9in × 6 in.)

ISBN-13: 978-1-64949-646-1 (paperback) | 978-1-64949-647-8 (trade paperback) | 978-1-64949-648-5 (e-book)

Key Words: Christian Spiritual Growth; Women's Bible Study; God's Will Study; Christian Worldview; Christian Living; Religion and Spirituality; Christian Bible Study

Library of Congress Control Number: 2022942133 Nonfiction

Dedication

For my children, Ross, Sam, and Mesa, and my daughters in love, Alyssa and Casey. May the Lord bless you in the holy journey chosen for each of you.

And for my nieces Kaycee and Laney. May the God of all comfort be so near, you'll never question his will for your lives.

And for my children's children, Ezekiel, Hazel, Benson, and Denver. And their children ... until he comes again, I pray God's beautiful will be revealed.

Teach me to do your will, for you are my God.
(Psalm 143:10)

Table of Contents

Acknowledgments

Thank you, Steve. Without your faith in God, we would not have had all these wild and wonderful adventures—some of which are told in these pages.

Thanks to my publisher, Deb Haggerty, for believing in this project. Thank you to the editors, the beta readers, and friends who have patiently read through many manuscripts out of selfless love. Without your support and sacrifices, *Bible Briefs* would be a dream in my head and not a reality on the page.

Set the Stage

"For it is God who is at work in you, both to desire and to work for His good pleasure." (Philippians 2:13)

God made you, loves you, and cares for you.

He provides for you too. And he protects.

He is a father, but also a pursuer who seeks to be known in a deep and intimate fashion.

He is so wildly enamored with you, so passionate about his relationship with you, he sacrificed his only son so he could dwell not only with *you* in eternity, but also on earth someday.

What kind of love is this?

It is an unfathomable love, beyond our human understanding, though we are called to try.

The most famous verse in the Word of God gives us a broad-daylight, uncover-the-secrets-look at this love:

"For God so loved the world, that He gave His only Son, so that everyone who believes in Him will not perish, but have eternal life" (John 3:16).

God so loves you ... and he so loves the world.

But there's more. Caring for you is God's pleasure, but he hasn't made you to be some glamorous diva eating bonbons from your crushed velvet lounge, wiggling toes at the nail tech in your Roman-columned corner.

No. This is not the picture God had in mind when he created you as the object of his affections.

You ... yes, you—the ordinary person who barely passed trigonometry. You, the one who started the dream job that turned out to be a nightmare. You, the creative soul who thought he'd be a novelist but turned out to be a part-time copywriter. You, the girl destined for the spotlight who ended up in the shadows, divorced and raising two kids on her own.

You, my friend, are God's secret weapon. God made you for great feats of glory.

Whoa.

What he made you for will change the lives of the people around you. What he made you for will change the world we live in.

This is why I've written *God's Will: Unraveling the Mystery Bible Briefs.* If you're stuck in the ordinary but aware of something more just inches from your fingertips, then I believe these studies were written for you.

But before we begin, I want to make sure what we'll cover makes spiritual sense to you. The Word of God is clear—without the Holy Spirit, we are unable to discern the deep truths of God. To have the Holy Spirit as your guide in truth seeking, you must first be saved.

So if by chance you've picked up this little guide out of Christian curiosity, let me take a moment to explain what becoming a believer in Christ means.

If you've read this far, chances are God the Father draws you to Christ (John 6:44). There will be no better time than now to let his love pull you in and accept his grace-filled offer as the propitiation for your sin. There is nothing you can do to earn this freely offered salvation. It is by grace—God's love—that he comes to you open-handed. You can start this acceptance by confessing sin in prayer, declaring your belief that Jesus died for your sins, was buried, and was raised from the dead, and trusting he (Jesus) is who he says he is—the way, the truth, and the life (John 14:6).

Let's do this now.

Boy, do I feel better, and I hope and pray you do as well. Even if you've been saved for ninety years, it's always good to look back on the simple act of salvation—a wonder of God's grace and love.

And if you've just confessed and prayed this prayer for the first time, welcome to the kingdom of God! I encourage you to find a church, be baptized, and join a discipleship program that is based on the Word of God.

Now we're ready to unravel the mystery of God's will. Not that his will should be a mystery to any believers in Christ. There are thousands of Bible verses that explain God's will for his children—from how we should live, to how we should love, to how we should serve.

But somewhere along the years of cultural adaptations here in the land of plenty, God's will has become about seeking personal gain and not a quest for truth. Many believe if you can find the perfect will of God and stay in it, cares and struggles will dissipate, and the pathway to success will open like a smooth highway leading to a pot of gold beneath an enchanted rainbow.

The opposite is true.

Once you're in God's will for your life, things will get messy. You'll find yourself dealing with humans who push back, question your sanity, and root themselves in some massive dead-end beliefs. There will be blood and flesh and guts everywhere while you are in his will. But operating in his design for a God-glorifying world, you'll find the sweet spot of elusive contentment. Joy and peace will be constant companions, and the superpowers of the spiritual world will be available to your previously ordinary self.

You'll experience peace in the chaos, confidence in the doubts, and God Almighty whispering in your ear along the way.

USING THESE BIBLE BRIEFS

My hope is that you'll slip these Bible Briefs into your already busy life. The point of the short three-lesson studies is to give you the opportunity to shape your Bible experiences to your current circumstances. There's no need to plan two hours a day for eight weeks, although you certainly can, if that's how you like to dive into the Word.

But you won't find weekly topics or daily directions. You're free to study when you want and how you want. And I encourage you to get messy with your notes, prayers, and struggles. Color, highlight, and write *Laurie, you are wrong on this one*, if you want. The more you interact with some of these new and coming thoughts, the more you'll emerge from the pages satisfied you've heard directly from the Lord.

Which is the point. As you'll find in these studies, discovering God's will isn't nearly as mysterious as we've often made it to be. He's taken the time and care to outline all that is on his heart concerning you within the pages of his Word. We've only to seek, and we will find.

Ready? I am!

"Do you not say, 'There are still four months, and then comes the harvest'?

Behold, I tell you, raise your eyes and observe the fields, that they are white for harvest." (John 4:35)

BEGINNINGS

"In the beginning was the Word, and the Word was with God, and the Word was God." (John 1:1)

Bible Brief 1

BEGINNNGS

THE FRAMEWORK

Somewhere along the path of my Christian walk, I happened onto the slippery slope of believing if the Lord was pleased with all my glittery efforts and spiritual accomplishments, I'd be in his will and blessed. There are several issues with this mindset, but the major problem with this theology was that *I* determined the definition of blessed. I defined this well-worn church word by American material standards: nice home, peaceful weekends, and how well my children behaved in various stages of life.

I'd forgotten those oft-overlooked Scriptures telling us to deny ourselves and pick up a cross (Matthew 16:24–26). I'd overlooked the Sermon on the Mount when Jesus said, "Blessed are the poor in Spirit ... blessed are those who hunger and thirst for righteousness" (Matthew 5:3–12). I'd ignored the biblical calls to be thankful in trials (James 1:2–4).

For me, there was a time when failed career plans, a drug-addicted son, and spiritual wrestling matches in the jungles of Africa were signs of God's displeasure, meaning I thought I operated outside his will.

The downhill slippery slope of my constant effort to do more and be more for the Lord was exhausting, yielding burnout instead of spiritual fruit. I trudged through these dry spiritual deserts, falling face down in the sands and mumbling the inevitable question: *What do you want from me anyway, God? And how the heck am I supposed to figure out your will for my life when everything is a mess?*

His answer, of course, was always with me. Buried in the thick book on my nightstand (and now digitized on my cell phone) were the simple, truthful answers to all the *whys* in my life. And once I began to study the book, answers came. Revelations didn't smack me in the head with mental two-by-fours, but answers came like a gentle rain for my dry, searching roots.

I found God's pleasure. And in finding his pleasure, I found my peace.

As he lifted me from the low desert sands to the high places of green pastures, revelations dawned, and I found my purpose walking in God's will, not the other way around.

So many times, I believe, we set our course determined and praying for God to bless our efforts. Of course we should pray, seeking God's favor and help in all things. But the simple spiritual shift for me was to seek his will first, *then* start the journey following him.

This is what happened when he sent my family to rural West Africa, calling my husband to work on a Bible translation project in Equatorial Guinea. I had reservations, but we stepped out in faith, not knowing God's complete plan or where we'd end up.

Where we ended up was back in the States with a family crisis just a year and half after moving to Equatorial Guinea.

Our faith trek seemed a failure.

But in those eighteen months tucked away in the wilds of Africa, the Holy Spirit undid my flesh and began to shape the person the Father initially designed when he created me.

And it was in all the trials in Africa where I found my purpose. Or rather I found God's plan for mankind, and how I could purposely fit into that plan.

You can fit too.

Acts 17:26 tells us God has appointed every person's time and geographical place. This means whatever he's doing in the current age, you were created to be here at this exact moment, living where you live.

The key that unlocks many of the mysteries of God is looking around and asking yourself, what is God doing in my life today? In my church today? In the world today? When the revelation comes, that's your invitation to join him in his work. Whether the work is in your personal faith growth, or your church's development, or in world affairs—and highly likely in all three—your job is to join him in what he is already doing.

He doesn't need *you* to create a strategy for him to bless. He's had a perfect plan for you to fit into his design since the beginning of time.

In this *Beginnings* study we'll investigate God's all-encompassing plans for the world, seeking the Holy Spirit to open our eyes to *his work*.

Hang with me as we start our studies with simple, well-known verses. As we pull these apart, as we look at them in context, I pray you receive fresh insight into the Father's glorifying plan for a people who follow him.

Buckle up. There will be mind-blowing revelations to ride.

Let's begin by building the framework of this first study:

"'I am the Alpha and the Omega,' says the Lord God, 'who is and who was and who is to come, the Almighty'" (Revelation 1:8).

While imprisoned on the island of Patmos, the apostle John received a lengthy vision of the fantastic but also gut-wrenching days ahead. John, acting as our Savior's scribe, recorded many things, including letters for the corporate church. As well, he chronicled visions of Christ and visions of the latter days, when the culmination of our purposes is brought to a glorifying moment at Christ's second coming. Near the beginning of this exciting and last book of the Bible, Christ tells John, "I am the Alpha and Omega ... the one who is and who was and who is to come" (Revelation 1:8). Alpha and omega are the first and last letters of the Greek alphabet. Jesus in essence says, I am all things first, I am all things in the in-between parts, and I will be the last—the pinnacle of the plans I've made for you.

This Bible Brief under the section *Beginnings* will deal with ... beginnings! To fully grasp all Christ has for us, I believe we need to understand his work in the past, in the days we live in now, and in the days to come.

We'll start with the past.

Lesson 1—Made Like Him

BEGINNINGS

"Everyone who is called by My name, and whom I have created for My glory, whom I have formed, even whom I have made." (Isaiah 43:7)

The opening statement of our Bibles says, "In the beginning God created the heavens and the earth." (Genesis 1:1)

After describing how light, earth, plants, and animals were created, and then stating his work was *good,* God is recorded as saying, "Let Us make mankind in Our image, according to Our likeness; and let them rule" (Genesis 1:26)

Profoundly, this account reveals what our Maker had in mind when he created the first humans—to be an image of our glorious God, operate in his likeness, and rule over all that he made—all that was good.

As people with biblical hunger, we are likely acquainted with these verses and could recite each word. But it is my desire that we look deeper than the familiar.

Let's peer beyond the words of the creation account and into *why* God orchestrated events and gave commandments in the ways he did, keeping in mind this first look at God's will lays the foundation for the rest of our revelation-exposing studies.

TAKE ACTION

Read Genesis 1:4, 10, 17, 21, 25, 31.

   1. What does God say about his work in each of these creation accounts?

_____

_____

_____

_____

_____

_____

Read John 1:1–3.

   2. Who was with God in the beginning?

_____

_____

_____

_____

_____

   3. All things were made through whom?

_____

_____

_____

_____

_____

_____

4. In your own words, describe what "good" means in the context of creation.

_____

_____

_____

_____

_____

_____

Read Hebrews 1:2.

5. Again, through whom were all things made?

_____

_____

_____

_____

_____

_____

God made man in his likeness. What could that mean? We look like him? We mirror his characteristics? We've been granted a free will? In what ways do we humans reflect God? In what ways do you personally reflect God? Write your thoughts on the next page:

_____

_____

_____

_____

_____

_____

_____

Looking back at the verses in John and Hebrews, I wish to establish Christ—the son of God, who was with God in the beginning—is the Creator. Later in our studies, we'll take a closer look at how the heir to the world has been involved in the plans for mankind right from the start.

But let's get back to Genesis and our creation account of the first people. In Genesis 1:28, we're told God made the first humans and then blessed them both—male and female. He said to them, "Be fruitful and multiply, and fill the earth, and subdue it; and rule over the fish of the sea and over the birds of the sky and over every living thing that moves on the earth." (Genesis 1:28)

DIVE DEEP

If you read through the entire account of creation, starting with Genesis 1:1 and ending with Genesis 1:31, you'll find God's first command to mankind is the above verse, Genesis 1:28. God made male and female humans, then immediately commanded them to be fruitful and multiply, fill the earth and subdue it, and rule over all within it.

Considering verse 31 tells us God saw and deemed all he had made as very good, then we know that goodness included both woman and man. God beheld the first people made in his likeness as *very good*.

Often what is *not* written in Scripture is as profound as what *is* written in Scripture. There are many, many commands God could have given to his first couple. *Don't take my name in vain,* or *do not lie,* or *don't partake in adultery.* But as sin infection did not yet exist, and everything God had made was good, the command took a different tone. He told his first, sinless humans to multiply, making *more* image bearers, and then he told these image bearers to go and rule *in goodness* over all that *was good*.

Sounds like a perfect world, right?

Here's the picture: good, image-bearing humans (righteous people) bringing God's glory to the good world he had made. God wanted a righteous people ruling over all he had made—all glorifying the Lord through his good work.

And there's more.

God not only wanted humans to rule his good earth and all that was in it, but he also desired they take part in the creation process moving forward.

Deliberate on this: With ample dust from the ground and a rib or two still available, God could certainly have populated the planet in the same way he created the first two human beings. But through his command and having been made in his image, humanity's purpose and desire was to multiply God's goodness throughout the earth.

As image bearers, we are to create even more image bearers and spread like holy, fruit-bearing vines across the earth.

Write your personal revelations from these Scriptures on the next page:

Lesson 1 Wrap Up

In other areas of the Bible, we are told God made man for his glory (Isaiah 43:7; 43:21; Revelation 4:11). As image bearers, we bring God glory as we multiply and subdue the earth, ruling over all God has made. As you ponder a goodly and godly-made man and woman subduing the entire earth, consider the areas you have subdued in the name of Christ. Write your thoughts.

Lesson 2—After the Fall

BEGINNINGS

"but from the tree of the knowledge of good and evil you shall not eat, for in the day that you eat from it, you will certainly die." (Genesis 2:17)

Adam and Eve are given their second directive soon after the first command, to multiply and subdue the good earth. You know the story. There are two trees in the garden of Eden they are warned not to eat from—the tree of the knowledge of good and evil, and the tree of life.

Along comes the father of lies in the form of a serpent, and he questions God's authority and purposes for Eve. His age-old temptation is an enticement I struggle with today— to be like God. I'm not saying I wish to be all-powerful or all-knowing, but I do have a sin nature that wants to be in control of a whole lot more than I need to be.

You?

After eating the fruit without any immediate consequence, Eve hustled over to her husband and said something like, *look, Adam … nothing has happened, and this fruit is really yummy.* She echoed the serpent by telling Adam *God*, in essence, *was a liar.*

The next verse tells us, "Then the eyes of both of them were opened, and they knew that they were naked" (Genesis 3:7).

TAKE ACTION

Read Genesis 3:7–24.

- The revelation of their nakedness caused the first humans to hide from God. What did God do to cover their nakedness?

_____

_____

_____

_____

_____

_____

Read Romans 5:9 and Hebrews 10:10.

- Today, who covers our shame?

_____

_____

_____

_____

_____

_____

We've mined the top layer of truth nuggets about God's plan for mankind. But while sin entered the *good* nature of man, God's purposes stood firm. A lying serpent could not alter God's plans or change his mind to have good image bearers multiply, go, and subdue.

Now sin-infused, Adam and Eve left the Garden, but they *multiplied*.

DIVE DEEP

Read Genesis 4:1–5:24.

The story of the first humans continues to be devastating. Adam and Eve, now sin-infected, conceived two sons. As the story goes, Cain, the firstborn, became a cultivator of the ground and his younger brother Abel became a shepherd—a keeper of flocks. In due time, both brought offerings to the Lord, but it was Abel's offering of a firstborn lamb from his sheepfold that the Lord regarded. We're not told the specifics of why Cain's sacrifice was disregarded (and I encourage you to read through different commentaries of conjecture on this story). Whatever the reason, Cain became angry and jealous, killing his favored brother. Cain committed the world's first murder, and we are told his brother's blood called to the Lord from the ground. God punished Cain, banishing him from the family to wander the earth, unable to produce crops from the ground. We're told Cain then left the presence of the Lord.

There's much to examine in this cryptic story of Cain and Abel, the first of the second generation of humans. But to keep us on our God's-blueprint-for-mankind track, we'll move on.

Despite this sinful blow to God's image bearers, multiplication and subduing began.

In your reading, make notes here of who builds cities and establishes territories:

_____

LESSON 2 WRAP UP

Sin could not stop God's plans. Now, with all of creation cursed, the purpose to create a glorifying race of humans to fill the creation stood firm.

Man faltered, not God's will.

Over the course of several Bible Briefs, we'll learn this initial plan to multiply and subdue for God's glory is the reason you're here, living in perhaps the most interesting days of human history—certainly the most gracious era to exist.

God's initial mandate for man was to go, to multiply, and to subdue all in his glory. God had not changed, even though man was now infected with sin. Can you think of a time when, despite your sin infection, God used you anyway?

Lesson 3—The Mandate Continues

BEGINNINGS

"By faith Noah, being warned by God about the things not yet seen, in reverence prepared an ark." (Hebrews 11:7)

The next major shift in early earth history is the story of Noah.

"Then the Lord saw that the wickedness of mankind was great on the earth, and that every intent of the thoughts of their hearts was only evil continually. So the Lord was sorry that He had made mankind on the earth, and He was grieved in His heart. Then the Lord said, 'I will wipe out mankind whom I have created from the face of the land; mankind, and animals as well, and crawling things, and the birds of the sky. For I am sorry that I have made them.' But Noah found favor in the eyes of the Lord." (Genesis 6:5–8)

With sin infecting the human race, Adam and Eve's descendants embodied evil, not the holiness of God. Humanity, meant to spread the image of our good and loving God across the world, spread the opposite—an evil, hideous image of a creation gone rogue.

And then God said, "Enough."

For forty days and forty nights the rain fell, covering the whole earth. Only Noah, his family, and thousands of pairs of living creatures survived in the ark. All else was destroyed.

TAKE ACTION:

Read Genesis 6:3–14; Matthew 24:37–39; Hebrews 11:7.

1. What was the earth filled with before the flood?

_____

_____

_____

_____

_____

_____

2. Do you see any similarities to the days of Noah and the days of our current world order?

_____

_____

_____

_____

_____

_____

3. The writer of Hebrews records Noah's faith, saying Noah believed what was not yet seen. With a sinful world all around, how would you have responded to

God's command to build an ark? Would you look at what is *not yet seen,* or would you depend on the news and rumors around you?

_____

_____

_____

_____

_____

_____

In my head, I can hear a few of you asking me, "What's the big deal here? You're covering the basics of the Old Testament, Laurie."

But this *is* a big deal. The familiar is what we most often overlook. In writing this *Bible Brief Beginnings*, I asked around, making sure it wasn't just me who hadn't swum around in the deep waters of God's command to multiply and subdue. I tested those waters.

I carefully selected three guinea pigs. My first question was: What was God's *first* command to Adam and Eve? Trying to trip folks up, I put a big emphasis on the word "first," hoping they'd say something about the forbidden trees. One hundred percent of the time, eyes rolling, their answers came: *Go forth and multiply.* One extremely biblically astute person added, "and subdue the earth."

Okay, I thought, I'm not very clever, but I didn't lose heart. I asked the next question: "Why?"

Ah-ha! I'd stumped two of them. Brows furrowed, their minds searching the internal files of old Sunday school lessons, they didn't have an answer. But the third person, who may or may not have been my husband, said, "Because God wanted to populate his creation."

I married up, and I know he's smarter than I am, but I pressed on. "Then why," I asked, "did God flood the world? If populating creation was the goal, then certainly the objective had been reached pre-flood."

"Sin," he answered.

"Yes," I agreed. "But if he wanted a sinless world population, then why not destroy everything, including Noah and his family, and start over? True, God called Noah blameless and in the New Testament we're told he had faith, but he certainly wasn't sinless. Later, in the New Testament, Paul tells us all men have sinned and fallen short of the glory of God." *All* includes Noah.

My husband mumbled something about giving him a headache. "Okay, then. You tell me," he said, reluctantly playing along.

I went for it.

"Our God wanted faithful people to multiply and subdue. That's a narrower target than vast humanity spreading far and wide. Noah's *faith* gave him the strength to believe God and build an ark. Faith is what God wanted to multiply back then, and faith is what God wants to multiply now. He seeks God-fearing, image-bearing people who, in faith, will show the world he is worthy."

My husband's proverbial light bulb lit up.

If you're asking yourself (or probably me) why these details are so important, I have an answer for you. Skipping ahead of our Old Testament multiplication lessons, read what Paul told the church in Ephesus.

"To me, the very least of all saints, this grace was given, to preach to the Gentiles the unfathomable riches of Christ, and to enlighten all people as to what the plan of the mystery is which for ages has been hidden in God, who created all things; so that the multifaceted wisdom of God might now be made known through the church to the rulers and the authorities in the heavenly places. This was in accordance with the eternal purpose which He carried out in Christ Jesus our Lord, in whom we have boldness and confident access through faith in Him." (Ephesians 3:8–12 emphasis added)

Wow. All along, God's plan to have a worldwide faithful people was for the purpose of making his glory and wisdom known ... through the church ... *to the rulers and the authorities in the heavenly places.*

Kingdom building to show other-dimensional beings what his wisdom and our faith looks like is why we Christians are here on Planet Earth today.

But we have to get back to the progression of man's multiplication failures, so we can see how faith would come to play the biggest part of the original blueprint. Let's go deeper.

DIVE DEEP

Read Genesis 7:1–24; 8:1–22; 9:1–2; 10:32; 11:1–9.

Interestingly, after the waters of the flood receded, and just as he did with Adam and Eve, God instructed Noah's sons to go forth and multiply, giving them authority over all creation.

But in chapter 11, the evils of man are recorded once more in the story of the tower of Babel. To force man to comply with his mandate to spread across the earth, God created thousands of different languages among the people so they could not understand each other or work together. Intent on spreading his glory across his creation, God created a multitude of languages so earth's inhabitants would separate and *go.*

In Genesis 11:4, the people are quoted as saying, "Come, let's build ourselves a city, and a tower whose top will reach into heaven, and let's make a name for ourselves; otherwise we will be scattered abroad over the face of all the earth" (Genesis 11:4).

It appears the people of the time, likely under the guidance of Nimrod (Genesis 10:8–13), had no appetite for God's plans to divide, go, and rule in his name.

His purposes have always and will always—until his millennial reign—include his people subduing the entire world for his glory.

The ancient historian Josephus documented that Nimrod had plans to build a sky-high tower, should God bring down the rains and drown the world again. By building a tower too high for flooding waters to cover, Nimrod would avenge his forefathers' deaths. From this historic account, it seems possible Noah's descendants lacked the faith to believe that God, after giving them a new covenant, would never destroy the earth by flood again. These faithless people didn't believe God.

In Genesis 11:8 we are told, "So the Lord scattered them abroad from there over the face of all the earth."

The Lord scattered them. The Lord made the way.
Record your thoughts from these passages:

LESSON 3 WRAP UP

Profound truth unfolds. God told the first Adam to go and multiply. He commanded Noah's sons to do the same. And when Noah's descendants refused, attempting to stop God from fulfilling his multiply-and-subdue plans, God created a way. That way produced more than seven thousand languages still living and being spoken today.

In light of the evil in the world today, have you been asked to build something (spiritual or material) that requires faith? What have you learned about God's blueprint for mankind?

_____

_____

_____

_____

_____

_____

_____

_____

Bible Brief 2

CALLED TO GO; CALLED TO BUILD

"The kingdom of the world has become the kingdom of our Lord and of His Christ; and He will reign forever and ever." (Revelation 11:15)

Bible Brief 2

CALLED TO GO; CALLED TO BUILD

THE FRAMEWORK

Since day one of creation, God's blueprint has been to build a holy kingdom of faithful earth dwellers. From Adam and Eve's original command to multiply and fill the earth, to Noah's descendants, to Abraham's call to move out and make a great nation, the idea has been that man should fill the earth with God-glorifying people.

But as I've stated in the first *Bible Brief,* I didn't completely understand what the Lord wanted from me. As I sought to understand the purpose of my being created now, in this time and space, I encountered detours.

I opened *Bible Brief One* with a personal story of how we stepped out in faith to work with a Bible translation project in Equatorial Guinea, Africa. Now I'd like to take you farther back, to the first time the thought of going to Africa ever entered my mind.

Years ago, while listening to Christian radio, I heard a pastor speak about personal desires. He said some people are hesitant to lay their entire lives at the altar of Christ, fearful they'll have to give up personal desires. This radio personality explained that Christ gives us the desires of our heart (Psalm 37:3–4). Those desires, he stated, are created by God in the first place. "So if you've been afraid to turn your ambitions over to the Lord because he might send you to Africa, no worries. If you don't desire to go to Africa, he will not send you to Africa."

Good, I thought. *The last place I want to be is Africa.*

Seven years later, I was in the middle of the Congolese Rainforest on the west coast of Africa with my husband and children, living without modern conveniences and wondering what happened to the promises of one zealous radio preacher.

I've come a long way since those eye-opening days in a foreign land. I've learned to turn to the Bible to decipher truth, not depending on teachers with the best intentions but slightly wrong theology. It may not have been my personal desire to live in the jungles of Africa, but it was certainly God's plan. There he taught me the need for God-glorifying multiplication in areas of the world yet to be subdued.

We'll come back later to my personal revelations. For now, let's get into the Word and see how God's world purposes include you and me spreading his glory.

Lesson 1—Building Nations for His Glory

CALLED TO GO—CALLED TO BUILD

"For what great nation is there that has a god so near to it as is the Lord our God whenever we call on Him?" (Deuteronomy 4:7)

Remember, before the fall of mankind, God revealed that everything in his creation—including humans—was good. But after sin infected the people, glorifying God with his creation looked radically different—and this *different* would exalt the Lord in ways those who called upon his name would *not* see coming.

Our Lord initiated a process of nation building that would have global implications and lasting significance.

The Maker patiently began by selecting Abram, a direct descendant of Shem, son of Noah, *to go*—to leave his home, relatives, and country behind to build a new and God-honoring nation.

TAKE ACTION

Read Genesis 12:1–3.

1. According to the Scriptures above, did Abraham know his destination?

----

2. Looking at verse 3, what is the purpose of Abraham's walk of faith?

The promise to bless all the families of the earth is our first glimpse at Abram's purpose in leaving his home. Not only were he and his descendants to be an example of a nation revering God, but in the promises of the above verses, this family and future nation would bring the hope of redemption to the whole world.

Again we see the Lord's concern with the world and *all* he has created.

On a personal note, I haven't always been affected with the world outside my own family or community. In my early Christian days of Bible studies, many of the lessons I gravitated toward focused on me—my calling, my self-esteem, my spiritual growth. I hardly noticed the world beyond my borders except in times of crises such as 9/11.

I'd missed the bigger picture of God's worldwide plans.

Personal growth is important. However, it seems some in the American church have camped out on this platform, focusing on the individual benefits of following Christ. Lessons on suffering, spiritual disciplines, and going into all the world are in short supply—unless you attend one of those rare but glorious churches that take in the whole Bible and not just the benefit plans.

Though Christ does dwell with you, and he certainly fights for you, his purposes as world creator include—well, the world. As his children, we are called to be concerned with the things that concern the Father, and according to Scripture, he is very concerned about the state of his creation.

God is passionate about the collective world he made.

DIVE DEEP

Read all of Genesis 17 and 18, noting when Abram's name is changed to Abraham. In Hebrew, Abram means *exalted father*. His changed name, Abraham, means "father of a multitude." The Lord is not only focused on building a nation for his glory but also in retaking the earth for his glory.

In chapter 18, God promises Abraham a son through his wife Sarah. Beyond child-bearing years, the elderly couple's faith is challenged. The Lord's response to their unbelief is one of the most quoted verses in the Bible (verse 14). He says, "Is anything too difficult for the Lord?"

The answer to this question is, of course, nothing is too difficult for the Lord.

The God who created the heavens and the earth, who brought about a world-destroying flood, who scattered people with seven thousand-plus languages can fulfill his promise to create a new God-infused, faith-wielding nation for his glory.

In verses 17–33, we're given insight into a very interesting conversation between Abraham and one I believe to be Jesus Christ, the personal manifestation of God. Right before Christ tells Abraham of his plans to destroy Sodom and Gomorrah, he looks to the two other angelic visitors with him and explains why Abraham has been chosen for the great task of nation building. He says, "For I have chosen him, so that he may command his children and his household after him to keep the way of the Lord by doing righteousness and justice" (verse 19).

To keep the way of the Lord. The manifested Christ explains Abraham's job is to command (teach and discipline) his children and household. Considering God has promised Abraham he will be the father of a *multitude* of nations (Genesis 17:4–5), we're shown again the Lord's bigger blueprint for mankind is to multiply and subdue the earth for God's glory. God chose a faithful man to go forth carrying the first command he'd given to Adam and Eve.

Record the passages that stood out to you in your reading assignment:

_____

_____

_____

_____

_____

_____

LESSON 1 WRAP UP

Our first glimpses of faith emerge from the stories of Abraham. From his calling to go forth into unknown places and his belief in the unseen promises, Abraham serves as a model of faith.

"By faith Abraham, when he was called, obeyed by going out to a place which he was to receive for an inheritance; and he left, not knowing where he was going" (Hebrews 11:8).

Sin had not kept our Maker from initiating his desire to fill the earth with God-fearing people. Keeping the Lord's world objectives in mind, how could you take a bigger role in the original blueprint for mankind to spread God's glory?

_____

_____

_____

_____

_____

_____

Lesson 2—Grace is the Way

CALLED TO GO—CALLED TO BUILD

"And I heard a loud voice from the throne, saying, "Behold, the tabernacle of God is among the people, and He will dwell among them, and they shall be His people, and God Himself will be among them." (Revelation 21:3)

From the time of creation to the calling of Abraham, some two thousand years passed. Interestingly, from the faith call of Abraham to the birth of Christ, the Bible records another two thousand years of history.

With a broad sweep of Scripture, let's review the struggles of the chosen nation, Israel.

TAKE ACTION

Read Exodus 29:44–46; 1 Samuel 8:4–22.

1. How did God's chosen people struggle? Make note of the problems that stand out to you.

_____

_____

_____

----

2. Why did God bring Israel out of Egypt?

God's purpose is clear. He brought Israel out of Egypt to be *among* the people.

"And they shall know that I am the Lord their God who brought them out of the land of Egypt, so that I might dwell among them; I am the Lord their God" (Exodus 29:46).

But after their Egyptian deliverance, the people of Israel lacked the faith to trust in the Almighty. Following a glowing cloud in the desert and eating manna falling from the skies required a strong unwavering faith. They probably felt more out of their element than I did in the jungles of Africa, where scientists still discover unknown creatures.

Perplexed with God's commands and obscure presence, the descendants of Abraham asked the Almighty for the familiar. They wanted a human ruler to lead them—not God.

Israel coveted the governments of other nations. Desiring what the heathen peoples had, the chosen people asked for a human king on a man-made throne. By doing so, Israel rejected God, denying the opportunity to have their Maker in their midst.

From that time, God dwelt behind the veils of their tabernacles and eventual temple, but rarely in their hearts. A moral king would rise on occasion, and faithful prophets would cry out to the Lord. But as a nation chosen to walk with God in righteousness and take that righteousness into the world, Israel fell short.

Like those before her.

The following years of Israel's struggle proved sin-infected man was incapable of reigning, ruling, or taking dominion over the earth for the glory of God.

Another failure? Another regret on God's part?

DIVE DEEP

Read Genesis 12:3; Micah 5:2; Isaiah 7:14; Daniel 2:44; Psalm 2:7; Malachi 3:1–6.

From Genesis to Malachi, over and over again the prophecy of a coming savior is foretold—a holy king destined to dwell among his people. A king who would not fail. A king righteous before God; a king to which every nation would at long last bow. As Israel struggled, the message of man's sin-infected failures became clear—by their own desires and works, man would never be righteous enough to nation-build a habitation for God.

I think of Eden, and how God walked in the garden before sin entered his creation.

But for the hope of a prophesied and coming king for Israel, all would have seemed lost. God had promised a coming Messiah, a ruler who would deliver Israel from her enemies and reign in the righteousness of God.

What the people of Israel didn't quite understand, however, was the scope of the promised king. Yes, he would rule Jerusalem in a future day. But this Messiah—

this God-infused, not sin- infected leader—would rule not just the Jews, but the world.

Write your personal revelations from the Scriptures above:

LESSON 2 WRAP UP:

I'm taking a thirty-thousand-foot view here and rushing through rich, rich Scripture to get us to the point of understanding that while God cherishes you (Zephaniah 3:17), he cherishes all he has made and is moving sinful mankind toward the culmination of something bigger than ourselves. His original desire to dwell in his creation—the world—has not changed.

In the next review, we'll discover how the resurrected Christ gives us the final mandate to go into every nation, spreading righteousness—filling the earth, reaching every nation, preparing the whole of creation for the return of a perfect, righteous king.

According to John 3:16, God loved the whole world and gave his only begotten son that whosoever believed in him would be saved. So far, has this study opened your eyes to a deeper understanding of how and why God loved the world? If so, write your thoughts:

_____

_____

_____

_____

_____

_____

_____

_____

_____

_____

_____

Lesson 3—The King Comes

CALLED TO GO; CALLED TO BUILD

"And Jesus came up and spoke to them, saying, 'All authority in heaven and on earth has been given to Me. Go, therefore, and make disciples of all the nations, baptizing them in the name of the Father and the Son and the Holy Spirit, teaching them to follow all that I commanded you; and behold, I am with you always, to the end of the age.'" (Matthew 28:18–20)

Today Christ dwells *within* those who belong to him. In a coming time, he will physically rule and reign among every people. Until the time of his physical return, we are to be kingdom builders, going into every people group and sharing the good news of Christ's atoning sacrifice, but also discipling, building up a community of believers who not only know him but who follow the righteous ways of the Lord.

But Christ's directive to go into every nation and disciple has become no more than a box to be checked off in the list of efforts from some of our mission committees. Going into the dark corners of the world and subduing for Christ isn't simply a suggested effort for the church. This is a mandate from God from the beginning, and a repeated mandate of Christ before his ascension. And there is an end game attached.

In 2017, a Barna Group survey produced a report claiming less than half of churchgoers in the United States were familiar with the phrase Great Commission. While the term is not used in the Bible per se, it is an expression used to describe Christ's call to evangelism found in all four Gospels including Acts, but most noted in the book of Matthew. If less than half of churchgoers in 2017 knew of this mandate, I can imagine with the chaos and crises of the past few years, we've grown less concerned with the biblical command to *go*, and more and more focused on the recommendations to stay. Going hasn't been easy to accomplish as the world shut down for a pandemic and wars broke out around the world.

The Barna report further showed only 17 percent of those surveyed were confident of the meaning of this church-age term. The data collected by Barna seems to indicate that the phrase—or more specifically, the work—has lost its priority within the Western church. This is a tragic revelation as evangelism—the sharing of Christ and the building of the church—is central to our earthly purpose. From the creation of man to the prophesied second coming of Christ, the Bible weaves a story of God's plan to dwell with a worldwide and holy people.

Since that day some long two thousand years ago, we've been bringing people into his kingdom, preparing a holy nation for the return of Christ.

However, the kingdom is far from filled. An estimated 1.5 billion people have yet to hear the Good News of Christ in a language they fully grasp. Millions of people groups still do not have a Bible translated into their language, and because seventy percent of the world's population lives and learns in predominately oral cultures, millions more still do not have audio Scripture in their language as an option.

More than two thousand languages still need a Bible translation, and some five thousand still need these translations put into audio because the people groups either cannot or will not read. Audio Scriptures are imperative for the nonreading majority living in the nations today.

There are very dark corners of the world still to conquer for Christ.

And the church seemingly has lost interest.

TAKE ACTION

Read Acts 17:24–27.

1. Where does God *not* dwell today?

_____

_____

_____

_____

_____

_____

2. Why did God make man and woman, determining where and when each would dwell?

_____

_____

_____

_____

_____

_____

Read Acts 1:6–8.

    1. In verse 8, the resurrected Christ tells his disciples they will receive the power of the Holy Spirit. From Jerusalem, where will they go to be witnesses?

_____

_____

_____

_____

_____

    2. According to the beginning of this third review in our study, have we yet gone to the remotest parts of the earth?

_____

_____

_____

_____

_____

    The revelation of God's Great Commission plans came to me while living down the dirt-road pathway of an African witchdoctor.

During our eighteen-month work in Equatorial Guinea, we had a church college group from the United States come for mission work, helping to build a cistern for our main campus (an acre of cleared-out jungle and a couple of adobe buildings) and initiate evangelism. During their week, the young adults visited neighbors, taking along guitars and inviting people to come to a presentation night at the end of the week.

After living among the people of Bata, Equatorial Guinea, for months, I knew getting these folks to come to a presentation would not be difficult. Because Americans always have food and money—the things village dwellers desire—people from miles away would show up for the treats. And with life conducted at the basic levels of survival, entertainment of any kind is bound to produce stories worth telling for years to come. They'll come, we reassured the college team. They will come.

I was right. Roughly two hundred people came to hear the young preachers and musicians.

The night buzzed with energy (and mosquitoes), and after an explanation of the gospel, the invitation to accept Christ rang forth. Many rushed forward, including the witch doctor who lived down the path from us.

While the young adults visiting from the states rejoiced, I held my breath. At that point, I knew Guinean culture enough to know these folks had hard lives, and you could get them to sign up for most anything with the promise of a better life ... or even a better meal.

Two days after the American group left, I set out to try and disciple a woman I'd seen raise her hand to accept Christ at the event.

On my way to this woman's side of the neighborhood, I noted the witch doctor dancing around in her front yard. She'd put up a cross, painted it white, and was chanting beneath it, throwing potions. She'd added our Christian symbol to her bag of magic tricks.

Oh, my.

With a native speaker in tow, I found the woman I'd seen and hoped to disciple. Her name was May. After a few simple questions about her understanding of the gospel, my heart sank. No, May didn't understand at all who Jesus was, or if he could really help her. She was desperate to have her son return home. The problem? A witchdoctor had turned May's son into a leopard, and he now roamed the jungle as a large cat. Then May told the translator she wouldn't talk with me about this any further because she knew I didn't believe in black magic.

She was right.

But *she* believed in black magic. And she wanted someone to help. May said, "Jesus did not help me. My son did not come home last night."

"What she needs," my translator patiently explained to me, "is for someone to read her a Bible so she can discover truth for herself. Then she will understand your reason for discipling."

Unfortunately the Bible had yet to be translated into her language.

This was an aha moment for me.

I'd heard the term *drive-by evangelism*, but now I saw the results. Few in this jungle hometown of mine had enough exposure to Christ to understand the purpose of an altar call. While I cannot judge the heart of any man, and I feel certain salvation did happen that night, I also realized discipleship and training (subduing) would take more than a two-week mission trip.

Using Christ as the ultimate example, we see how discipling for the sake of bringing people into the kingdom is done: for three years, he ate, traveled, and slept among those he discipled.

To subdue, we must stick around long enough to conquer the fear and the lies Satan has spent generations establishing. Discipling nations for Christ is no quick stop to an exotic, faraway land. Discipling nations for Christ requires sacrifice in almost every area of our lives. Kingdom building across the world is a hard, messy job, but it is the desire of our Savior that we do this—that *we* prepare a world for his return.

DIVE DEEP

Read Isaiah 46:9–11; Daniel 2:22; Matthew 13:17; Revelation 7:9–11.

Through his Word, God reveals the purposes of a multitude of mysteries. In Matthew 13:17, Christ tells us that before his physical walk on earth, prophets and righteous people longed to understand these mysteries. Even as he spoke to those around him at the time, they did not yet grasp his death would happen in a matter of days. Yet Christ continued to teach, comfort, and point to heavenly truths through parables and by quoting the Old Testament.

How wonderfully revelation comes—through study, prayer, and listening. It is with these disciplines that we respect and appreciate the spiritual revelations as they unfold.

Christ's sacrifice on the cross, foreshadowed by the first blood sacrifice in Genesis for Adam and Eve, was another mystery revealed.

But praise God, he does not wish us to walk around in a cloud of obscurity. He tells us the end of all things from the beginning.

In Revelation 7:9, we are shown the results of our Great Commission (Matthew 28:18–20) efforts. On the island of Patmos, the apostle John was taken into another dimension and time and there he saw representatives from every nation, tribe, and tongue before the throne of Christ. More than seven thousand language groups.

God, in his grace and love, showed John that the mandate to go and fill the earth and subdue through discipleship will be completed. Every language group, splintered at the tower of Babel, will come together in a future God-glorifying day. Write your revelations or thoughts:

_____

_____

_____

_____

_____

_____

LESSON 3 WRAP UP

From Genesis to Revelation, we see God's passion to build a kingdom—a community of righteous people who rule and reign over his entire physical creation. At the head of that community is King Jesus.

Today we build the kingdom. Tomorrow a kingdom comes where Christ sits on an earthly throne, and we, the global church, rule and reign with him—a time foreshadowed by the garden of Eden.

This will be the culmination of some six thousand years of our Lord's work through mankind. You are living in a time and place, chosen for you, to kingdom build. We start building through our families, move on to our communities, and ultimately into the world. Kingdom building is accomplished through prayer, supporting missions and groups who serve in communities, and the Great Commission work happening around the world today.

Interestingly, there are worldwide mission agencies working together today to finish Great Commission work. For the first time in history, every language group has been identified and the plans to disciple with God's Word are in play. Working closely together and charting the final stretch, these agencies have identified 2033 as the possible time when every nation will have access to God's Word in a language and format that speaks to the culture.

Our generation could be *the* generation to finish up the first mandate to *go*.

This, my friend, is exciting news. All glory to God, as his plans cannot be thwarted.

Living in West Africa, I came to understand the need for discipleship and the part God intended for me to play. Though our time in the foreign land had been cut short because of family trauma, in a year and half, I learned much about another world in need of God's truths. The Lord reshaped my calloused heart and put my sights on the world.

We were not able to return to Africa. Our family trauma became a years-long crisis, dealing with a drug-addicted son. We prayed through many hard times, and while I felt like a parental and missional failure, I still prayed for the world to know the truth. The world had stolen my son. I longed for that coming time when the earth again would be good and ruled by a righteous king.

So convinced of God's will for us to build a kingdom, preparing for his earthly reign, I prayed the Lord would give me a ministry to the world. Despite the messiness of my life, I wanted what I knew the Lord desired of me.

Now, I work stateside for an international ministry that shares God's Word in audio in the languages of the world. I have a front row seat to Great Commission work around the world, and I am excited to tell you the Word today spreads truth faster than Satan spreads lies. It's happening. It's real.

Praise God!

Bible Brief 3

EYES OPEN

"Open my eyes, that I may behold wonderful things from Your Law." (Psalm 119:18)

Bible Brief 3

EYES OPEN

THE FRAMEWORK

In the previous Bible Brief, *Called to Go,* we considered the worldwide overarching plan of God to fill the earth with his purified people, and create from every nation and tongue a kingdom which he would rule in the manifestation of Christ. A worldwide kingdom in which he would dwell.

We also learned his plans unfold through people and circumstances. This, I believe, is why we are called to be watchful—to be awake, fully alert, watching as the players on the world stage shift and signs emerge. If we are digesting the Word of God, and we are watchful for his plans, then we are given the wisdom to experience revelation.

Being transparent here, I will confess I've asked God to send me an email before. One with bulleted to-do lists or directions. I've wondered why he doesn't make my seeking his daily and life-long will easier or faster. *Wouldn't it be more efficient to just tell me how to or why to, Lord?*

But where's the relationship in typed words on a flat screen?

As when Jacob wrestled with the angel of the Lord (Genesis 32:24–32), we, too, must pursue this passionate, sometimes messy relationship with the One who put his breath in our lungs. When Jacob refused to the let the angel go, demanding a blessing, the angel said, "Your name shall no longer be Jacob, but Israel; for you have contended with God and with men, and have prevailed" (verse 28).

It is in contending and prevailing that we come face to face with our fierce-as-a-lion but gentle-as-a-lamb God Almighty.

And so we must wrestle through some of the hard to understand and even harder to execute commands found in the Word of God. Trusting in this relationship, we'll be exposed to his purposes.

It is our Maker's will that we know what he is doing and what he wishes to accomplish. In the last study, we looked at Isaiah 46:9–11. Here it is:

> Remember the former things long past,
> For I am God, and there is no other;
> I am God, and there is no one like Me,
> Declaring the end from the beginning,
> And from ancient times things which have not been done,
> Saying, 'My plan will be established,
> And I will accomplish all My good pleasure.

He declares to you and me the end of all things from the very beginning of all things. No surprises, no gotcha moments. In our supernatural connection, he is open-handed with his heart. A relational deity, God reveals who is he is, why you exist, and what the future will look like.

But there is a caveat. We must come and behold. We must watch and be awake and attentive to not only who he is, but what he's doing in the world all around us.

> The Lord of armies is with us;
> The God of Jacob is our stronghold. Selah
> "Come, behold the works of the Lord,
> Who has inflicted horrific events on the earth.

He makes wars to cease to the end of the earth;
He breaks the bow and cuts the spear in two;
He burns the chariots with fire.
"Stop striving and know that I am God;
I will be exalted among the nations, I will be exalted
on the earth."
The Lord of armies is with us;
The God of Jacob is our stronghold." Selah
(Psalm 46:7–11)

Lesson 1—Do You Not See These Things?

EYES OPEN

"But beware; I have told you everything in advance."
(Mark 13:23)

As an adult, I recommitted my life to Christ.

I'd had a salvation experience at a young age. To be honest, I had two salvation experiences. Or so I thought at the time.

First, I went through Girls in Action (GA) discipleship classes with the First Baptist Church in Waxahachie, Texas. At the end of these classes, and during a church service, my heart stirred to follow Christ. I'd learned about him and knew I wanted to be in his family. I answered the altar call and some weeks later, after meeting with the head pastor, I was baptized.

But a couple of years later, during a corporate revival at the same church, the guest evangelist gave a powerful message on Christ's forgiveness. I remember the clarity of understanding what Christ had done on the cross. The revelation came to me in a new way—my heart began to pound. My body started to shake. Before I knew it, I'd stepped out from the pews hosting my preteen friends, and somehow got all my trembling parts down the aisle again. In tears, I explained to the deacon helping with prayer that I needed to be baptized again. "It didn't take the first time," I cried. "I have to do this."

You can imagine the pot I stirred.

My mother was contacted, the head pastor was called, and meetings commenced. *Do you understand that Christ died once for all sin?* they asked. *Did you know what you did during the first baptism?*

I really didn't know much except I one-hundred-percent wanted Christ to be my savior. If I had to be dunked twice, so be it.

Eventually, everyone concluded I was in fact saved, the first baptism worked, and I'd simply had an emotional reaction to the powerful preaching of the visiting evangelist.

Whatever. They can call it what they want, but I know that I know what I know. It was in the second trip down the aisle that I ran into the arms of my Savior.

My walk with Christ has been an adventure since that day.

Except for the blind years. I call my teens and early adult years the blind years because, as is the case with many of us, I let the cares of life take control as I ran headfirst into adulthood, rarely checking my rearview mirror of better judgment.

Somehow, as is his way, while I exercised my own will, Christ stayed close, never completely turning me over to the world I so desperately wanted to be a part of.

But as I said, once the Lord said *enough* and pulled this wandering lamb back into the fold (and that's another wild story), I recommitted.

Zealous for truth and hungry for the Word, I joined any Bible study group who'd take me. I read the Bible consistently, and signed up for all kinds of committees at church.

But in all the incoming information, love, and support, something ... something was missing. I couldn't put my finger on it, but I felt a little like a person in the dark, moving from unknown room to unknown room, searching for a light switch.

You see, because I was curious, I'd listen to all kinds of teachings. At the Bible Church in town, I received solid biblical instruction. But on the radio and TV shows I tuned into, I'd hear other theologies—things that didn't totally line up with the grace of God. Some radio sermons taught about prosperity and how God's will for us was to be rich and happy. I thought theology was one big conglomeration of whatever I needed it to be, whenever I needed it. It was a pretty convenient way to walk with the Lord.

Today, this is what we call syncretism—the fusing of different doctrines to fit our current needs.

But by God's grace, one day I read the story of Solomon. The request for wisdom from David's son—heir to the Davidic throne—resonated with me. Wisdom? I hadn't thought about it before. I'd only sought God's blessings for my own, whatever the problem was at the time. But seeking wisdom? Would God grant me supernatural insight? What if I could begin to understand God's will and serve him through a deeper relationship?

I pondered Solomon's request for wisdom for a day or two, then took the plunge. I got a journal and a pen and sat cross-legged in the middle of my bed, my husband wrapping up the day with our kids.

I prayed. In earnest, I asked God to give me wisdom.

I won't say when I opened my eyes I felt like an all-knowing sage. I still had questions, and today I continue to wrestle with knowing God's complete and perfect will.

But I did notice a little change here and a big revelation there. Scripture would come to me when I needed to give an account for the Lord. Or when I wrote a ministry newsletter, I could exposit somewhat using a Greek or Hebrew lexicon. I got over the surface, feel-good teachings and felt pulled to the commentators of old, studying eighteenth and early nineteenth-century teachers. I experienced two-way prayer instead of the typical cover-my-personal-list-then-say-amen talk at God.

After the prayer for wisdom, I began to talk *with* God.

I'm still Laurie. I'm still zany, goofy, and inquisitive. I still trip over my own feet and get those feet in my mouth plenty. But when I speak to audiences or write for studies like this, fresh new revelation can come out of the blue as I flip through the pages of my worn NASB Bible.

That's God's wisdom and understanding pouring over me.

And it's the most exciting experience ever. There's nothing in this material world like having spiritual puzzle pieces fall into their right slots. I liken the experience to being very thirsty, bent over and peering into a deep, dry well, when suddenly the well is not just overflowing with water, but it's filled so full, it's splashing up on me and I am left completely saturated, hair dripping and thinking, how did *that* just happen?

So let's peer into a water hole that might have been dry for some time—the ability to discern all the God activity around us. I think by the end of this study, you will have experienced a little water-dowsing from what we thought was a dry well, but in reality is a river of bubbling, gushing water.

Here we go.

In the books of Matthew and Mark, we're given an insider's look into a fascinating exchange between Jesus and his twelve disciples. The discussion begins when the disciples, walking through the streets of Jerusalem, point out the majestic temple building, probably bragging about the stately temple built to honor ... well, Jesus, the guy standing next to them. As Christ addresses these men with likely puffed-up chests, he almost sounds exasperated. He says, "Do you not see all these things?"(Matthew 24:2).

Then he announces in a future day, the temple will be destroyed.

But the question *Do you not see all these things?* begs looking into.

Before this temple scene, Christ had encountered a group of Pharisees who wanted to test his claims of deity. They asked him to show them a sign—proof of who he claimed to be—from the heavenly places where God dwells. To their lack of faith, Jesus replies:

"When it is evening, you say, 'It will be fair weather, for the sky is red.' And in the morning, 'There will be a storm today, for the sky is red and threatening.' You know how to discern the appearance of the sky, but are you unable to discern the signs of the times?" (Matthew 16:2–3).

Again Jesus answers a question with the question, "but are you unable to discern the signs of the times?"

Jesus seems perplexed that those who claim to know God hadn't yet figured out who he was or the world-changing strategy about to develop.

The tragedy here is all along the prophecies of Christ were discernable to those who studied Scripture and sought God's wisdom. Let's turn to the Word and see how we know this.

TAKE ACTION

Read Psalm 111:6, 10 and Proverbs 2:1–5.

1. Who has God made his power known to?

_____

_____

_____

_____

_____

2. How are we to obtain the understanding of his power?

_____

_____

_____

_____

_____

3. Who does God store up sound wisdom for?

_____

_____

_____

_____

_____

Read Psalm 119:26–28, 33, 66.

1. These Psalms reflect the servant in prayer. What is this psalmist asking for?

_____

_____

_____

_____

_____

_____

In Psalm 119:27, we see the writer making a declaration about what he will do once he has understanding. What is that action?

_____

_____

_____

_____

_____

_____

Read Ephesians 3:20 and 1 John 5:14–15.

- When we ask within the will of God, what is the answer?

_____

_____

_____

_____

Read Psalm 119:28–30; Proverbs 2:6; Psalm 119:9–16.

   1. What strengthens the psalmist?

----

   2. What is treasured in the writer's heart?

Read John 16:13.

- Before Christ was crucified, buried, and raised again, what promise did he leave his disciples?

_____

_____

_____

When we seek the wisdom and understanding of the Lord, we are granted our requests. Throughout the Psalms and Proverbs, the writers ask the Lord over and again to bestow these supernatural gifts.

If we wish to discern spiritual mysteries, we must first ask God for the ability.

As well, God's Word imparts wisdom. Look back at Psalm 119:9–16. These meditations and prayers are rejoicing in God's Word and ordinances. As you take in the Word, pray for wisdom. God generously grants what he's always wanted us to have—the inside scoop on his perfect will.

DIVE DEEP

Read Ephesians 1:1–14.

Family secrets are entrusted to family members. So it is with God. His secret ways and understandings are reserved for family members—believers in Christ. Through these verses in Ephesians, we discover family members are blessed with every spiritual blessing in the heavenlies. These blessings have been available since the foundation of the earth—since the first call to go forth and multiply and subdue.

Through Christ, we are lavished with wisdom and insight and the riches of grace. In verse 9, we're told God has made known the mystery of his will through Christ.

His will has been made known. It's there, waiting for you to reach for it.

How fantastically amazing that we have a treasure more valuable than gold or silver—the shared understanding and knowledge of the God of the universe (Proverbs 16:16).

And through our studies, we've already discovered God's will for you and for me is to go forth (share the gospel), multiply (bring believers into the kingdom), and subdue (disciple as we prepare for the return of Christ).

Write the insight you've gained from studying Ephesians 1:1–14 here:

LESSON 1 WRAP UP

Psalm 25:14 says the secret of the Lord is for those who fear him, and he will make them know his covenant. James 1:5 tells us if we lack wisdom, we are to ask for it, never doubting the Lord of every good and perfect gift will grant this request. His will is there, working in your life, your family, your community, and our world. We simply have to seek it, ask for insight, wisdom, and understanding, and watch as the answers unfold not only through the Word but also through life.

My prayer is when we encounter Christ at his second coming, he'll have no need to ask, *Did you not see these things?*

As we keep our eyes open to all the Lord has done, is doing, and will do in our lives and world today, we begin to understand his will, joining him in what he is already doing. Look around. Where do you see God working in your situations now?

_____

_____

_____

_____

_____

_____

_____

_____

_____

Lesson 2–Prophecy Matters

EYES OPEN

> "The scepter will not depart from Judah, nor the ruler's staff from between his feet, until Shiloh comes, and to him shall be the obedience of the peoples." (Genesis 49:10)

Now that we know we can possess discernment and be equipped with knowledge and understanding, let's look at what it means to be watchful.

As we discussed in the opening of this *Eyes Open Bible Brief*, Jesus seemed perplexed when neither the Pharisees nor his disciples appeared to understand the true plans for the Messiah. Prophesies of a coming Messiah were told and foreshadowed through circumstances and events in the Old Testament.

A well-known example of this is the story of Abraham. In obedience to God, Abraham placed his beloved son Isaac on an altar of sacrifice, willing to slay his prophesied son as a sacrifice to the Lord. Here, Christ was foreshadowed as the sacrificial lamb.

Another but perhaps lesser-known example of foreshadowing is the story of Melchizedek, the priest who blessed Abraham (Genesis 14:18–20). Some four thousand years later, the writer of the book of Hebrews (5:1–7; 7:1–28; 8:1–6) explains how this mysterious priest who stepped out to bless Abraham was a foreshadow of Christ's permanent holy, priestly position.

Throughout the Psalms and through the writings of the Old Testament prophets, signs of the coming Messiah are recorded.

TAKE ACTION

Read Psalms 2:1–12; 8:6; 18:49; Isaiah 42:1–4; 49:1–6; Hosea 11:1; Micah 5:2.

- Consider each prophecy. How did these prophecies point to Jesus Christ?

_____

_____

_____

_____

_____

_____

The above Scriptures by no means represent an exhaustive list of prophetic signs or prophetic declarations of the coming Christ. Conservative estimates put the total number of fulfilled Messianic prophesies near three hundred.

Christ confirms prophecy fulfillment when in Luke, after his resurrection, he walks with two of his disciples on the road to Emmaus. As the men speak to whom they believe is just another man, they tell this man of Christ's death and their disappointment—they had believed the Jesus they spoke of would be the one to redeem Israel.

Christ replies, "You foolish men and slow of heart to believe in all that the prophets have spoken!" (Luke 24:25)

Jesus then begins to explain to these slow-of-heart men the prophesies that were written about him.

Oh my. I hope we begin to understand the depth of what takes place in these passages. These words are not merely accounts of a story that happened, but revelations into God's heart. He wants us to understand, to have the wisdom to see beyond the obvious and into what he's doing.

In the previous studies, we learned our God is relational. Here's a recap of what we know of God's relational character:

- It is his desire to dwell among men—righteous men, and he's made his desire known from the beginning (Exodus 25:8).
- He foretold his plans for man's redemption (Genesis 3:15) because he wants us to know him and his plans.
- Our Maker willingly reveals his world-altering plans with us (Isaiah 46:10).

DIVE DEEP

In the context of this *Eyes Open* study, it's important to understand the purpose of prophecy. There's going to be some Bible page-flipping in this section but hang in there. All the Scripture below is related to being alert and watchful for what the Lord God has done, is doing, and will do. Some of these verses explain why prophecy is important, while others are prophetic in nature. Like other Scripture lists I've placed in these studies, the following is not an exhaustive account of staying watchful. But I think you'll begin to better understand the importance of knowing and seeing what God is doing and why watching is his will for you.

Read Deuteronomy 28:15, 28; Mark 13:23; 2 Timothy 3:16; Hebrews 1:1; 1 Peter 3:15; Ephesians 1:9–10; Ephesians 3:8–12; Colossians 4:2–6; Matthew 26:41; Luke 21:36; Mark 13:33.

As miners searching for sparkling gold or silver beneath the obvious grays of ordinary rock, we can uncover dazzling truths when we dig deep into the Word.

Fulfilled prophecy confirms God is all in all. Fulfilled prophecy reassures us what he speaks about the future will come to reality. He can be trusted. He doesn't give in to the whims of human nature or change course to please peers. He doesn't forget his professed objectives or his promised outcomes. He is a rock-steady, firm-foundation, never-changing Father. And we, living among the impulses of other humans, can have a hard time buying that absolute truth. But this is what faith is all about.

After reading and then contemplating the above Scriptures, assign those verses you feel support the statements below:

- As righteous image bearers, we're not to grope in darkness.
- As kingdom builders/multipliers, we are to speak of his salvation clearly.
- As rulers over his creation, we are to prove God trustworthy.
- As believers, we are to prove the inerrancy of Scripture.
- As God's children, we are to watch our Father work in the world.
- As God's children, we are to be prepared for his work results in all seasons.

LESSON 2 WRAP UP

Our Maker took immense care to foretell his first coming. The majority of those who claimed to know God missed the prophesies foretold by the prophets. Christ's exasperated-sounding response to his followers and spiritual leaders of the day, *do you not see these things* (Matthew 24:2), lets us know they should have.

Throughout history, God's plans and his generous heart have been revealed. Are we paying attention today? If so, we'll discover not only his will for mankind, seeing where he works, but how we can be involved.

As we understand how prophecy has been fulfilled in the past, we can place greater confidence in his promises for today and tomorrow. We can watch with great expectation, reading the signs and preparing for what's next in the prophetic calendar.

Take time to pray through these revelations. Should prophecy matter to you? Why or why not? Write your thoughts here.

_____

_____

_____

_____

_____

_____

Lesson 3—Slow of Heart

EYES OPEN

"You foolish men and slow of heart to believe in all that the prophets have spoken!" (Luke 24:25)

As we move into this final *Eyes Open Bible Brief*, I'd like to revisit the reason I wrote this study: I'm not a prophesy fanatic. I'm a *God's purposes* fanatic.

Let me explain with a story.

Once the Lord took me to Equatorial Guinea, stripped me of modern conveniences, showed me what society without him looked like, and revealed the lack of truth accessible to roughly 1.5 billion people (more people than live in the whole of the Americas, including Greenland), I began to dig through my Bible in search of answers. I wanted to know *if* the depravity and false religions engulfing these people could possibly be his will. And if it was his will, how had I escaped the same plight?

Turning to the Word, I discovered the truth—as he will be exalted among the nations, it has never been his will for these people to be without truth. As well, I hadn't been chosen to live the blessed life. I'd been chosen to use my blessed state to join God in subduing the world for his glory.

As I wrote in the previous studies, his will is to make his dwelling place among the people of the earth. For a good part of my life, I'd been taught Jesus wanted to live *in my heart*, but oh, how little I was taught about his desire to live in *and* among his creation.

While I'm still a very self-centered person of the flesh, after reaching these Great Commission conclusions, I added God's concerns to my personal list of concerns. He has great passion for the bibleless people we worked among in Africa. It has never been his will that these people live without knowing him, the truth, and the opportunity for grace-filled salvation.

After only eighteen months in Equatorial Guinea, we returned to Texas seeking help for our drug-addicted son. There I found it harder to relate to what had once been my people group—my church community. My theology had shifted. Comparatively, after sitting on a backless bench under a palm-tree ceiling with one simple drum accompanying *a cappella* singers in Africa, the $10,000 sound system overhead in my American church seemed extravagant. After witnessing people beg for the Word of God in their own language, I found the average four Bibles (various versions) hosted in the American Christian home shocking. What had once been my trophy of spiritual growth—multiple Bible tools—was now my shame.

I've leveled out over the years, realizing that when I live in the land of plenty, I am a part of the culture. A judging or bitter heart is not productive to kingdom work. I determined to live as an American but to keep God's priorities at the center of my Christian walk. It's true, I have a nice home, car, and still have multiple Bibles at my fingertips. But my prayers, my work, and my financial giving have changed radically.

Understanding the Great Commission is more than an exercise in sending those peculiar people in our congregations to other lands to handle the messiness of cross-cultural evangelism. Great Commission work is long-haul commitment—sharing God's Word, long-term discipling, and preparing all nations for the return of Christ. And this massive job will require the passion of all God's children.

In another change experienced from my short time in the mission field, I began to watch for God's work in nations and current events. I found myself more interested in the future than I did the present. Scriptures validated my passion for preparing for the Lord's return:

"[I]n the future there is reserved for me the crown of righteousness, which the Lord, the righteous Judge, will award to me on that day; and not only to me, but also to all who have loved His appearing" (2 Timothy 4:8).

So with my passions blazing, I'd talk on about the signs of the times as if every Christ follower ought to be interested. Time and again, I'd be met with this statement: *No one knows the day of the Lord's coming … Laurie (name said with contempt).*

At least folks knew this much of Christ's prophetic discourse found in Matthew 24 and 25. The interesting thing about their statements is they leave off the command part of the verses. Here's the whole enchilada:

"Therefore be on the alert, for you do not know which day your Lord is coming" (Matthew 24:42).

"Be on the alert then, because you do not know the day nor the hour" (Matthew 25:13).

Clearly, we're to be alert *because* we do not know. We've not been given the date, so we're to be watching, knowing the season and the time are near. It amazes me how people take this verse and project the opposite of its valuable meaning. I've been told, in essence, to not look for Christ's coming because ... if he'd wanted me to be concerned, he would have let me know the exact time of his arrival.

That's some crazy talk.

And false theology.

But the craziest response I've ever had to my now more carefully placed pearls (Matthew 7:6) of prophetic, watchful comments is the one I had recently with a staff member from my work. When I mentioned the prophetic times we live in and how, biblically, signs were lining up in and around Israel, he said, "My theology on the second coming is this. Lots of people in the past have thought we were close to Christ's return, and they were wrong." He shrugged. "I'm not going to worry about it."

What?

So other people being zealous but mistaken determined his view of the biggest event in history—the reason the world was made? Or was he being lazy to say, *eh, it must be hard to discern ... so I'll pass.*

If he'd gotten his theology from the Word of God, and not from other people's misinterpretations, he might have found the Lord has an awful lot to say about his children being watchful, eyes open, and focused on what he's doing today and in the future.

Let's jump in and take a look.

TAKE ACTION

Read Colossians 4:2; Matthew 24:42; Mark 13:33; Luke 21:36; 1 Thessalonians 5:6.

- What do these verses have in common?

_____

_____

Read Matthew 13:10–16

   1. What is the topic of this conversation between Christ and his disciples?

---

   2. Why does Jesus speak in parables?

---

   3. Who in these verses does Jesus call blessed?

_____

_____

_____

_____

Being watchful, alert, and awake are all powerful words, intended to get our attention.

As in his statement about the coming false religions (Matthew 24:5), Jesus warns his disciples of the prospect of being misled. He is a compassionate king, letting his own know of the perilous times ahead.

If you read Matthew 24 in its entirety, you'll find more warnings and signs. There is no question, Christ wills that we are not caught off guard as the culmination of God's worldly plans come together. If we are to be about our Father's business, then we must know what and when his business is.

In trying to relate all that's going on in these Scriptures, I think about my relationship with my husband and how we communicate. We're avid gardeners, and in this specific season of life, I'm working full time and writing as a side job. My garden time is limited, but my husband continues to care for the multiple plants and landscaping around our house.

At the end of a Saturday, I go out to see his work. I am always interested to observe how he's reshaped a tree, pruned a bush, transplanted seedlings. We discuss the progress and what work has been reserved for my hands. I get excited about the end product—how our growing gardens will take shape and eventually provide wonderful shade from the New Mexico desert sun, and luscious blooms for our visual enjoyment.

Is this not how God asks that we relate to him—to watch for his work, ask to join him in the process, and anticipate with great eagerness the final kingdom—the result of his blueprint for mankind?

DIVE DEEP

Read Matthew 24:32–51; 25:1–13.

Matthew 24 and 25 are full of amazing revelations. In the above Scriptures, Jesus uses parables to teach about his second coming. In the parable about the fig tree, he explains that when we see those first, tender leaves sprouting from the branch, we know summer is near. It is the same with prophecy, he reveals. When we begin to see the events prophesied in Matthew 24:4–31, we will know Christ's return is near.

Christ's discourse takes his listeners from the fig tree parable to a warning—telling the disciples that the coming of the son of man will be like the days of Noah, unexpected and sudden.

The next parable is the one emphasizing Christ's command to be prepared. He begins by saying, *be on alert, for you do not know which day your Lord is coming.*

Be on alert.

Why?

He explains.

In Matthew 24:43, Christ likens his return to a thief entering a house, saying, "if the head of the house had known at what time of the night the thief was coming, he would have been on alert and would not have allowed his house to be broken into."

We may not know the hour or day of his return. But we can know the season. Christ expects us to understand, through signs and careful Word study, the season of his return.

Next up—the parable of the ten virgins. You know the story. Five virgins are prepared with oil for their lamps, five are not, and these five unprepared virgins are not allowed into the wedding feast. Again Christ ends this parable with the words, "Be on alert then, for you do not know the day nor the hour" (Matthew 25:13).

Clearly, being watchful leads to preparation. Prepared status is not simply a warning from our Maker, but a command.

Because we've camped out in chapters 24 and 25 of Matthew, I feel it's important to note a prophetic verse pointing directly back to God's original world design of spreading his glory.

"This gospel of the kingdom shall be preached in the whole world as a testimony to all nations, and then the end will come." (Matthew 24:14)

Passionate for the nations, his return to rule will be closely connected to our work in going and building and spreading his glory.

LESSON 3 WRAP UP

We should be concerned with what concerns our God. And since the culmination of his worldly plans are in Jesus Christ ruling the earth, we should focus on the big stuff.

Is the Lord interested in our daily lives and the trials a broken world pours on our heads? Yes! Much of Paul's teachings in the New Testament are about discipleship—how to respond to and endure the trials. But we are made in God's image, which means we are able to face the troubles of the world *because* we have hope for the world—because we have the answers.

When my personal ambitions hit a dead end, I can become discouraged. When the son who struggles with addictions loses a battle, I can even get angry with God.

But thanks to hope and mercy, all these situations are temporary. I'm reminded that Christ returns and throws Satan into an abyss, chained for a thousand years (Revelation 20:1–3).

What about you? Are you able to cling to the rugged hope of the future? In light of what we've discussed in this *Eyes Open* Bible Brief, will you be able to keep your sights on the bigger picture of God's plans for the world? Write your thoughts here:

_____

_____

_____

_____

_____

_____

_____

_____

_____

_____

_____

Bible Brief 4

HE MAKES IT PERSONAL

"These things I have spoken to you so that My joy may be in you, and that your joy may be made full." (John 15:11)

Bible Brief 4

HE MAKES IT PERSONAL

FRAMEWORK

According to Scripture—the truth the Lord has equipped us with—our purposes lie in knowing and following Christ. He is the one who came as a revealing light, ripping veils and scattering the shadows. The mysteries of El Shaddai (God Almighty) are revealed but also fulfilled in the coming of the God-man, Jesus Christ.

If you've read the previous studies, you are now aware there are unreached people groups in the world still today. There is Great Commission work to be accomplished.

But there are also unreached areas of our minds, as we've allowed culture to shape how we think and believe about God and his plans for us. There is disciplined work of the Spirit that needs to be accomplished in our thoughts and beliefs.

The Word of God transcends cultures, whether it's the me-first society which has shaped God to be a vending machine waiting on our personal requests, or the disconnected culture that reflects an aloof and uncaring God. Neither are true.

God is at work at all times. He works in the world to bring about the culmination of his material-world plans, and he works in you and me to fit our desires and dreams into these plans.

He is a working God.

His work in and through you is not about fulfilling *your* plans. It's about fulfilling *his* plans for you.

But somehow we've allowed our industrious culture to shape the idea that our gifting and callings equate not to kingdom building but to career successes and personal desires realized.

I know because I've been there.

In this last study of *God's Will: Unraveling the Mystery*, we will revisit the who, the how, and the what of our individual callings, clearing a mental and spiritual path for the Lord's anointing power to flow through.

Here we go to revelation. He'll make it personal.

Lesson 1—The Who of Your Calling

HE MAKES IT PERSONAL

"For we are His workmanship, created in Christ Jesus for good works, which God prepared beforehand so that we would walk in them." (Ephesians 2:10)

At forty-something and living in an underdeveloped area of Africa, I struggled with drastic changes in every area of life. In missionary circles, these struggles can be called culture shock. Culture shock usually hits in the first six months of living in a new country and can spur the newbie to anger or despondency. I experienced both.

Unable to communicate well with anyone other than my family and two other missionaries we served beside, I wrestled with isolation.

Having worked years in a family business, having been the founding director of a crisis pregnancy center, a cofounder of a maternity home, and a writer and public speaker, I was used to taking charge of situations and making things clip along at American speed. Life in Equatorial Guinea moved along at a much slower pace, and I discovered the control I had flirted with in the US was an illusion.

I couldn't take charge of anything in Equatorial Guinea. Even homeschooling my children felt foreign. I worried I'd scar them for life. To this day, one of them blames me for her poor grades in geography because my idea of geography class was putting together one of those colorful puzzles of the United States.

Lord, I tried.

Before reading a missionary cookbook produced by Wycliffe Bible Translators, I thought cooking consisted of dropping a Pop-Tart into the toaster. Where we lived in the Congolese Rain Forest, there were no Pop-Tarts. Or toasters. We had electricity only a few hours a week, so all three meals for all the mouths around my table were up to me and my prowess in the kitchen.

Not only was I concerned about my ability to provide a quality education for my children, but I also worried I'd starve them to death.

I flunked kitchen. I flunked school-teacher mom, too. And language acquisition class.

I failed Missionary 101 right in the big middle of our lives as missionaries.

In frustration one day, I locked myself in the bedroom with my journal and Bible. I told the family to not come near the bedroom door.

Wide-eyed, they backed away.

Inside, I spent a couple of hours moaning to the Lord about my career, my purpose, and how there wasn't a place for me to use the gifts and talents he'd so graciously bestowed on me back in the US. In the hot, humid jungle, the only thing I did well was sweat.

Our gracious Lord uses every hard situation to mold us—to shape us closer to his image. And he used the challenges in Equatorial Guinea to teach me important lessons about callings and his will for me. Later in this study, I'll come back to the story of how I emerged from my bedroom spiritually beat up, but with a whole new perspective of why and who I was.

But for now, let's allow Scripture, and what the Lord has to say about his individual calls, to reshape our thinking.

TAKE ACTION

Read John 15:16. According to this Scripture, what are we chosen to do?

_____

_____

_____

_____

_____

_____

Read Hebrews 13:20–21. What is pleasing to God?

_____

_____

_____

_____

_____

_____

Read 1 Thessalonians 5:24. When the Lord calls you into service, who accomplishes *his* will? Write your thoughts on the next page:

_____

_____

_____

_____

_____

_____

Reading through John 15, I am struck by the reality of God's choosing. Jesus makes it clear *he is the one* who appoints us. Discovering this appointment is no mysterious search in the shadows, for just as God has made his active work known to Christ, so Christ has shown us what the Father does.

Your appointment will be in tandem with what and where God is already doing or working. He is the master vinedresser, already working in the vineyard. You are the tiny new branch called to bear fruit. And the process is pleasing to the Lord God, the vinedresser.

Isn't this great news? Just as I cried out from my African bedroom to the Lord, through Scripture he revealed that because *he worked* in this foreign African land, I was called to bear fruit there. It didn't matter I hadn't mastered being a geography teacher or could not fluently speak the multiple foreign languages coming at me. It didn't matter that I felt inept at doing even the simplest things. He would be the one to do the work he desired accomplished.

He, as we shall learn later in this three-lesson *He Makes it Personal*, would be my source of power.

It would be through his choice and his strength that I would bear fruit.

DIVE DEEP

Read Jeremiah 1:4–10

Even though these recorded verses are a conversation between Jeremiah the prophet and God Almighty, in reading them, insightful truth emerges. God is able, from the time we are formed in our mothers' wombs, to appoint us for his purposes. We are crafted with purpose in mind.

Even when Jeremiah says, *what ... not me ... I'm no good at speaking ... I'm too young for this kind of gig,* God answers, *you shall go where I tell you and you shall speak what I command, and I will be with you.*

The pressure was off. Jeremiah had only to follow God's commands. No blueprint strategy to graph, no extra college classes on public speaking, no knocking down church doors. Jeremiah's assignment was to watch and listen for the Lord and to speak up when the Lord said to do so.

These fascinating truths opened for me in the bedroom that day in Equatorial Guinea. When I whined about not using the gifts he'd given me, the Lord replied, "Exactly."

Through more prayer and Scriptures reading, he showed me I was right where he wanted me to be. He didn't need me speaking, writing, or birthing a new ministry. At that moment—in a hot, humid jungle, where I was unable to effectively communicate with neighbors or church members and questioned my purpose in it all, the Lord impressed upon me that he didn't *need* me to do anything. He *desired* that I see what he was doing in the dark corners of the world. *Wait and watch, then join me,* he said.

If he was willing to show me what he was doing, then I could trust he would invite me into his work. I was where I was supposed to be.

"Sit down," he told me. "I have things to show you."

Often, God's will for us is to simply sit down.

"And ordering the crowds to sit down on the grass, He took the five loaves and the two fish, and looked up toward heaven. He blessed the food and breaking the loaves, He gave them to the disciples, and the disciples gave them to the crowds" (Matthew 14:19 emphasis added).

Lesson 1 Wrap up

In John 15:16, we learned we don't choose our purpose. The Lord chooses his purposes for us. And in Jeremiah 1:4–10, we discovered the choosing may well happen before our infant eyes ever see the light of day. First Thessalonians 5:24 states it is God who will be faithful to work through your calling and in the calling, he will accomplish his will.

This is no mystery. God's will for your life unfolds as he guides you into areas where he is working. He will press upon your heart his passion for the lost sheep in the world, the growing of new believers, and the work of the body of Christ, the New Testament church.

Although I do some writing and speaking today, I also work with an international ministry that shares God's audible Word in the languages of the world. After seeing people in oral cultures who had Bibles they couldn't read, God showed me how he would work through his recorded Word in audio. Through an adventure that could have only been God, I've ended up working in the very need he exposed me to back in Equatorial Guinea.

The gifts of speaking and writing were not to be used for my own edification or career enhancement, but for bringing glory to his work in the vineyard.

Whether you're traveling a dusty road in the desert of no answers or sitting in green fields being fed by the hand of Christ, you are where you are supposed to be. Unless you are obviously outside God's will through sin or selfishness, then you are where you are supposed to be—available for the Lord's purposes.

No matter the circumstance, the first step in unraveling the mystery of God's will is to buy into the truth—hook, line, and sinker. He is sovereign over all, including your purpose.

In the next lesson, we'll study the *why* of your calling—why God chose you to be his reflection and witness to an unbelieving world.

Lesson 2—The Why of Your Calling

MAKE IT PERSONAL

But we all, with unveiled faces, looking as in a mirror at the glory of the Lord, are being transformed into the same image from glory to glory, just as from the Lord, the Spirit. (2 Corinthians 3:18)

Through years of working in nonprofit Christian ministry, I've interacted with people who believed they were in God's perfect will. Others feared they were outside God's elusive will. Still others questioned God's sovereign will or assigned his will to their career choices. Some of their God's-will crises were legitimate valleys of struggles, designed by the Lord to build faith. Some were self-inflicted, painful seasons of doubting their calls, because their promotion or raise never came. Then there were others who understood how God's will is to be part of everyday abiding life—the simple *and* the complex—with the Holy Spirit guiding them from one unique challenge to the next.

I believe it is wrong to assume if things are coming your way in an easy fashion, this is proof you are operating in God's perfect will. I also believe it is wrong to assume if circumstances turn sour, this is proof you are outside God's will.

And yet, both the above situations can be indicators from our guide, the Holy Spirit.

How does one know the difference between those red lights to stop and the green lights to go? Read the following Scriptures:

> So Jesus was saying to those Jews who had believed Him, "If you continue in My word, then you are truly My disciples." (John 8:31)

> "Remain in Me, and I in you. Just as the branch cannot bear fruit of itself but must remain in the vine, so neither can you unless you remain in Me. I am the vine, you are the branches; the one who remains in Me, and I in him bears much fruit, for apart from Me you can do nothing." (John 15:4–5)

> "My sheep listen to My voice, and I know them, and they follow Me." (John 10:27)

In John 15, Christ uses the beautiful metaphor of a grapevine to explain how we abide in him. Because he is the sturdy vine, he not only supports the various branches, but he is also the source for the nutrients flowing from the roots to the branches. Spiritually speaking, it is his power that flows into us, giving us the ability to be fruit bearers.

A branch cannot hop on and off a vine. A branch grows out of the vine *because* of the nourishment flowing from the vine. The above Scriptures guide us into this truth: When we abide through the study of the Word and through the disciplines of prayer and meditation, we will bear fruit, which is God's perfect will. Fruit-bearing is God's purpose for you. Fruit-bearing is God's will for you.

Here's the miracle: While abiding, you can and will bear fruit in all circumstances.

Therefore, the question shifts from *what is God's will for our lives?* to *how do we bear fruit in every way possible? How do we abide?*

The answer? By allowing Christ's spirit to flow in the hard, the glorious, and the dull circumstances in life. Lay your personal agenda down and let the power, moment by moment whisper in your ear.

TAKE ACTION

Read John 15: 1–11.

1. Who is the true vine?

_____

_____

_____

_____

_____

_____

2. Who is the vinedresser?

_____

_____

_____

_____

_____

3. What does the vinedresser do with fruitless

branches?

_____

_____

_____

_____

_____

_____

4. What does the vinedresser do with fruit-bearing branches?

_____

_____

_____

_____

_____

_____

5. What is the result of painful pruning?

_____

_____

_____

_____

_____

_____

6. Who is glorified when we bear more and more fruit?

_____

_____

_____

_____

_____

_____

Read Genesis 1:28.

   1. What was God's command to the first humans?

_____

_____

_____

_____

_____

_____

   2. Once fruitful, what were Adam and Eve to do?

_____

_____

_____

_____

_____

_____

My point in Lesson Two of *The Why* of your personal call is that his will is about his glory. Your *why me, why now?* is answered in two words—his glory.

The Lord's will is not focused on our professional careers, our children's sports achievements, our political views, our wealth, our health, our pantries, or our wardrobes.

However, he absolutely cares about all these areas of life and is more than aware of what we need (Matthew 6:25–33).

But his grand *purpose* for you is not an end game. It's life-long mirroring of his glory, always bearing fruit, always pointing to him.

You were born to bring him glory.

In essence, everything you do should point to the glory of God. From your income-producing job, your interactions at the grocery store checkout, your homeschool co-op, your golf game, your prayer life in the secret places—all these things are opportunities to glorify the Lord.

DIVE DEEP

When we glorify him in all, then he calls us and entrusts us with more and more opportunity. The increase in opportunity is a result of glory stewardship. Read through the parable of the talents found in Matthew 25:14–29. This parable outlines how the Lord increases our opportunity when we use what he's given us to increase his glory; to increase what is important to him. And as we've learned in the previous studies of these Bible Briefs, God's will—his original blueprint for mankind—is to increase the glorifying kingdom which he plans to inhabit.

LESSON 2 WRAP UP

"I can do nothing on My own. As I hear, I judge; and My judgment is righteous, because I do not seek My own will but the will of Him who sent Me" (John 5:30 emphasis added).

"For I have come down from heaven, not to do My own will, but the will of Him who sent Me" (John 6:38 emphasis added).

Like Jesus, we are each called to seek and accomplish the will of God. If there's doubt and uncertainty when it comes to knowing the Lord's purpose for you specifically, there's a good chance the flesh and spirit are in a wrestling match. In my personal life, I've had many aspirations—some have panned out, some have not. What I've learned, through the lessons the Lord's brought, is if I'm bearing the fruit sanctioned by the vine, then I am living and moving in the glory of the Lord, reflecting him to those within my influence, no matter the circumstance.

I don't wish to dismiss specific callings. Like each of the twelve disciples called to follow Christ for three years, and like Moses, Esther, and Abraham who were placed in specific locations to bring about God's will in unique situations, we each will be called to step out in faith at a crucial moment. If you abide—when that time comes—you, like the sheep of the shepherd's flock, will know his voice and will be called out to do a mighty work. And likely that work will require sacrifice.

But, oh, the glory that will come.

 Lesson 3—The Spiritual Gifts

MAKE IT PERSONAL

Who saved us and called us with a holy calling, not according to our works, but according to His own purpose and grace, which was granted to us in Christ Jesus from all eternity. (2 Timothy 1:9)

We've learned we are called, not according to our works, but according to his purposes. And like the branch on the mighty life-giving vine, we are to bear beautiful fruit. This is God's perfect will.

A grapevine has many branches, spreading across the vineyard. You, as the branch, are only part of the greater vineyard picture. As we'll see in the coming Scriptures, you've been gifted with special spiritual gifts to keep the vineyard healthy and spread the glory of God.

But first a personal story.

Having been employed in Christian ministry for nearly thirty years, I've encountered people who were filled so full of the Holy Spirit, their bodies practically glowed from the glory reflected from the Lord. Wise, kind, and patient, these people never sought a glory of their own. They treated their ministry seasons as gifts from the Lord.

These giants in the faith bore glorious ripe fruit, ready for the picking in season and out.

I can characterize these godly men and women as patient, listening, loving, and always pointing to the Lord as the reason for it all.

I've also encountered people who had their theology mixed up, using Scripture out of context to support whatever their flesh had in mind for personal gain. One such example happened when I worked as a fundraiser, traveling around the country to meet with supporters of a particular ministry. I'd experienced supernatural success in raising funds, knowing the Lord used specific gifts he'd bestowed. But one day, when discussing future fundraising plans, a coworker said, "God has anointed you to bring in money for this ministry, and you'll likely be approached by other ministries with job offers because of your success. But you need to know, he has anointed you for *this ministry* and if you leave, the anointing will not follow."

Say what?

My coworker's manipulative statement was not biblical. Though we may be called to a specific position or job, God will not remove our giftings when he moves us to another place. Because he works through people and circumstances, it's likely he'll move you around, shaping you in new situations and using your gifts in multiple conditions. There are instances where people spend a lifetime working in one specific area, but my coworker's comments were meant to instill fear, not faith.

We are called to bear fruit, to go, and to multiply. Granted, these wide-vision callings can look a lot of different ways, but to say our gifts are only useful in certain circumstances is not the truth.

Here's what God's Word has to say:

"for the gifts and the calling of God are irrevocable" (Romans 11:29).

I do not wish to take this verse out of context, so I remind myself that in this eleventh chapter of Romans, the apostle Paul speaks of Israel and how, though she has not come into a national belief in Christ, we are not to scorn her. God's will for Israel will come to pass. But the principle of God's assignments is there in the verse. God's gifts are irrevocable. Moving from one job, one work, one labor to another does not nullify a supernatural gifting of the Lord.

And we each, according to God's grace, have been given a spiritual gift for several purposes.

TAKE ACTION

Read Acts 1:8.

1. After receiving the gift of power, what were the disciples called to do?

_____

_____

_____

_____

_____

_____

2. Where would the disciples take their gifts?

_____

_____

_____

Read 1 Peter 2:9–10.

   1. As people unified in Christ, how does Paul describe us?

----

   2. For what purpose has God chosen you and me?

Read 1 Corinthians 12:7–11.

   1. Who determines our giftings?

_____

_____

_____

2. Why are we given specific spiritual gifts?

_____

_____

_____

_____

_____

_____

Now that we've determined it is the Holy Spirit's choice to equip us with a unique spiritual gift for the purpose of edifying the church and becoming a holy nation for God's glory, let's look at the biblically documented gifts of the Spirit.

Romans 12 lists seven gifts. They are the gifts of exhortation, giving, leadership, mercy, prophecy, service, and teaching.

First Corinthians 12 names thirteen spiritual gifts. They are the gifts of administration, apostle, discernment, faith, healings, helps, knowledge, miracles, prophecy, teaching, tongues, tongues interpretation, and wisdom.

Ephesians 4 lists five: apostle, evangelism, pastor, prophecy, and teaching.

Each gift listed above, we're told, is for the *common good* (1 Corinthians 12:7). Each serves as a tool to support the greater body of Christ for the greater purpose. While the gifts can encompass a career, such as pastor or evangelist, most are used voluntarily in seeking to further

God's encompassing blueprint for the world—the mystery of Christ and the church, the royal priesthood building up a holy kingdom.

Our giftings are not derived from any natural ability or special education.

DIVE DEEP

Read through Romans 12 and ponder the instructions Paul gives to the church in Rome. I'm challenged by the underlying but consistent call to use our spiritual gifts in love and humility. In a culture that values titles, it can be challenging to not seek or accept the praises of men. I know I struggle with this very common desire of the flesh. We're taught from a very early age to identify what we want to be when we grow up in the way of career or title, and that's just the beginning of the problem. Throughout our young lives we're geared toward man-made educational systems, wrapping our lives around jobs, security, bank accounts, and a coming retirement.

What if we did it differently? What if we taught sacrifice, love, and kingdom building were to be first in life planning?

Try and imagine the world as God planned it—as it will be when he returns. Write some of your wildest wishes for this kingdom here:

_____

_____

_____

_____

_____

_____

LESSON 3 WRAP UP

Have you taken a spiritual gifts inventory or test? These tests can help identify your personal spiritual giftings and point you to a supernatural fulfilling role within your church body. But my suggestion comes with a warning. In taking these exams, it's easy to apply your current job or position while exploring the gifts.

When I led a women's ministry at church, we took a suggested spiritual inventory. One of my friends scored high in the gift of administration, and she happened to work as a top-level hospital administrator. I immediately asked her to serve with me in organizing our many events and getting the spreadsheets I'd neglected up to date. She agreed, but over time, the details she was supposed to be gifted to accomplish got pushed aside. She spent her free time sitting at the bedsides of the sick, with a special draw to those in hospice or near death. She was a comfort in the storms of suffering humans, a rock in the shifting sands of other people's lives.

I finally had my *aha* moment and realized she'd scored high in administration because it was what she did all day. Of course she was excellent in this area. But her *spiritual* gift to edify the body of Christ was mercy. In mercy, she was pulled to be with the discouraged, the sick— those preparing to leave this world and enter the next. She was and is today a blessing to many hurting people.

We shifted our roles around and began to pray, asking the Lord to *show* us how he'd gifted our women instead of depending upon a man-made test.

That being said, I'm not discounting spiritual inventories, but encouraging all to be watchful for unexpected gifts to emerge among the chosen of God.

Years ago, my pastor did this very thing with me. As I wrote earlier, I was the founding director of a crisis pregnancy center in Texas. During the early years of those days, Pastor B, I'll call him, shared an office space with me while his office at the church building was under construction. After listening to me on the phone with anxious women and girls who called in one day, he said, "Laurie, you have the gift of faith. It's in every conversation you have."

I'd never considered my gift was faith, because sold-out, unquestioning belief was who I had been for a couple of years. I'd assumed every Christian operated in strong faith. Once identified by Pastor B, I felt a supernatural freedom to speak up and encourage people, reminding them God was faithful and in total control.

As our Lord gently guided me in and out of experiences, including the days in Africa, he continued to build my faith.

Along with Scripture study, my faith has grown, and this is how I know without a doubt the Lord will return to a holy people who have, in passion and love, prepared a kingdom for him.

So let me encourage you. You are involved in an historical plan which will climax with the return of Christ. You are part of a holy nation, a member of a royal priesthood. You have been given every tool you need to prepare for the coming, glorious day when the love you've been sensing and experiencing all these years stands before you in the flesh as a holy king.

I can't wait!

Amen.

Bible Brief

FINALE

But seek first His kingdom and His righteousness, and all these things will be provided to you. (Matthew 6:33)

Finale

Matthew 6:33 sums up everything we've wrestled through in these studies. Before seeking what we shall eat or drink, or how we should dress, and a host of other things that make our days anxious, we are to first seek his kingdom and his righteousness.

Until the epiphanies I experienced in Africa, I didn't understand exactly what Christ meant by seeking the kingdom first. I understood seeking righteousness—becoming a mature disciple, turning away from my sinful nature. But seeking his kingdom? Was I to go to the heavens? How would I get there, except by dying? Was the kingdom I was to seek a secret place, one I could mentally teleport to? I racked my brain asking, *which kingdom are you talking about, God, and how do I seek it?*

But now—now that I've put my own will to the side and chased after God's will, I've discovered seeking the kingdom means seeking all things Christ as he prepares to return to an image-bearing people—to dwell among and love.

We're to seek the will of God, which is all about his glory-giving kingdom.

This is God's will for you as an individual and also as part of the corporate body of Christ.

And through abiding in Christ as branches to the vine, we bear God-designed fruit, a necessary step in glorious kingdom preparation.

In the *Called to Build* study earlier in this guide, I mentioned the radio preacher who assured his listeners— me included—God would grant the desires of our hearts, because it was God who put those desires there in the first place. The well-meaning pastor wasn't completely wrong in his theological approach. There are plenty of Scriptures that speak of the desires of man and how God will bless these plans. Here are a couple for review:

"Delight yourself in the Lord; and He will give you the desires of your heart" (Psalm 37:4).

"The plans of the heart belong to a person, but the answer of the tongue is from the Lord. All the ways of a person are clean in his own sight, but the Lord examines the motives. Commit your works to the Lord, and your plans will be established" (Proverbs 16:1–3).

Notice the writers of these Scriptures mention a condition for receiving the fulfillment of our personal desires. In Psalm 37:4, that condition is to delight ourselves in the Lord. In Proverbs 16:1–3, the condition is to commit our works to the Lord *before* those works are established.

These conditions are not legalistic contracts where, if we say the right prayer at the right time, we can convince God to act on our behalf. What the writers tell us, I believe, is when our motives are in line with God's motives, we can be sure our efforts will be blessed. We can rest in this promise because as we've already learned, it is the Lord who not only wills our directions but works through us to accomplish that will.

To help me better understand how I get my heart to line up with God's desires and passions, I look to a beautiful passage where God explains to Ezekiel the importance of having his name glorified among the nations:

> Therefore say to the house of Israel, "This is what the Lord God says: 'It is not for your sake, house of Israel, that I am about to act, but for My holy name, which

you have profaned among the nations where you went. And I will vindicate the holiness of My great name which has been profaned among the nations, which you have profaned among them. Then the nations will know that I am the Lord,' declares the Lord God, 'when I show Myself holy among you in their sight. For I will take you from the nations, and gather you from all the lands; and I will bring you into your own land. Then I will sprinkle clean water on you, and you will be clean; I will cleanse you from all your filthiness and from all your idols. Moreover, I will give you a new heart and put a new spirit within you; and I will remove the heart of stone from your flesh and give you a heart of flesh. And I will put My Spirit within you and bring it about that you walk in My statutes, and are careful and follow My ordinances. (Ezekiel 36:22–27)

Did you catch the part about the new heart?

God knows that within our original hearts lie selfish motives that don't reflect his character or his will. To Ezekiel, he referred to our hearts as hearts of stone. But he promises to cleanse us, put his spirit within us, and give us a new heart—his heart—so we can walk in his ways.

The new heart and spirit are prepackaged with the Lord's desires.

If you've accepted Christ as Savior, then yours is a new heart, beating in rhythm with God's desires. Step away from the noise of your culture and listen to that still, small voice. You will find as you delight yourself in the Lord and commit your ways to him, the natural flow will be having his plans already established in your heart and in your life.

I'm not sure about you, but I find this truth very exciting. Any fruit I bear depends upon the Lord's work in and through me. If fruit-bearing were up to me, I'd likely have the same results as homeschooling and cooking in Equatorial Guinea. Disaster.

But thank God! He accomplishes all.

Final Thoughts

As we began this study at the beginning of the Word, we should finish with the truths found in the end, in the book of Revelation.

Revelation (*apokalupsis* in Greek) means to *remove the cover*. In this last book of our Bible, we're given an insider's glimpse at what the days before the earthly reign of Christ will look like. God's will has been made known from the beginning to the end, and as his children, we are equipped with not only the power to accomplish his will, but with discernment to watch world events unfold just as he's planned, knowing how to respond in his will.

In his hands, we are his secret weapons.

I know because we accomplish all, *all*, he intended for us. He wrote it down in chapter 20 of Revelation:

> And he [the angel] threw him [the dragon, Satan] into the abyss and shut it and sealed it over him, so that he would not deceive the nations any longer, until the thousand years were completed; after these things he must be released for a short time.
>
> Then I saw thrones, and they sat on them, and judgment was given to them. And I saw the souls of those who had been beheaded because of their testimony of Jesus and because of the word of God, and those who had not worshiped the beast or his image, and had not received the mark on their foreheads and on their hands; and they came to life and reigned with Christ for a thousand years.
>
> Blessed and holy is the one who has a part in the first resurrection; over these the second death has no power, but they will be priests of God and of Christ, and will reign with Him for a thousand years. (Revelation 20:3–4, 6 emphasis added)

Christ will reign over a glorious world for a thousand years. You and I will experience perfect governance and a perfect love for mankind at last, the will of God fulfilled, and the nations worshipping the Lord.

Amen.

Oh, how I pray this study has given you a new perspective of God's will and how to operate within it. Through the Word, I hope you've learned he has carefully spelled out his desires, purposes, and how the future kingdom is the culmination of his original plan for mankind.

Go forth. Multiply the Christ followers. Share the good news with the nations. Bear fruit in all seasons, and abide with the Lord, my friends. The end, we're told in 1 Peter, of all things is near.

> After these things I looked, and behold, a great multitude which no one could count, from every nation and all the tribes, peoples, and languages, standing before the throne and before the Lamb, clothed in white robes, and palm branches were in their hands (Revelation 7:9).

$$\mathcal{Bible\ Brief}$$

STUDY GUIDE

STUDY ALONE WITH THE HOLY SPIRIT

Bible Briefs are formatted to fit your need. If you've got a day to dive in, you will likely finish the three lessons in one topical study. If you want to stretch your study time out, the lessons are short and can be accomplished daily in forty-five minutes to an hour. You can lay the study down to ponder, or pick it up, going for it until you're tired.

IN GROUP

These Briefs are also ideal for group gatherings. Whether in person or in an online group format, each lesson has questions that can lead to discussions. I recommend you review the Scriptures in your lessons and discuss answers in the *Take Action* portions. You may also have each person share how they answered the question at the end of the Dive Deep sections.

Here are a couple more questions to spur discussion:

- What stood out to you during your study time?

- Do you now see any of the Scriptures in a different light? From a new angle?

- Can you think of any other Scriptures that might fit into the lesson?
- What do you plan to do differently considering what you've learned about God's will?

To end a Bible study well, it's good to challenge the participants to apply what they've studied and plan for a follow-up time to discuss how their applications have played out. Have each member state or write how the studies have had an impact even weeks after the studies were completed.

At Brave (www.lauriegreenwestlake.com), we want to write relevant studies and blogs. If you have a topic you'd like to know more about, or see a need for a specific topic of the Bible, please write us at info@lauriegreenwestlake.com

Thank you. Be blessed as you journey in God's perfect will.

About the Author

L. G. Westlake is a wife, mother, and passionate student of the Word. For the past twenty plus years, L. G. has served in fulltime Christian ministry. Her services have included founding a Crisis Pregnancy Center, leading women's Bible studies, serving and teaching in multiple countries, and working in leadership with an international ministry. She has also written award-winning spiritual novels and multiple articles for Christian publications. But whether speaking to truth seekers or writing from a heart of passion, L.G.'s deepest desire is to make apologetics—the defense of God's Word—joyfully contagious. You can read more of her writings at www.LaurieGreenWestlake.com

OTHER BOOKS BY L. G. WESTLAKE

Made in the USA
Middletown, DE
05 August 2022